Lewis & Clark

The Missouri River

John Hamilton

Ogden School LRC
501 W. Ogden Ave.
LaGrange, Illinois 60525

VISIT US AT
WWW.ABDOPUB.COM

Published by ABDO & Daughters, an imprint of ABDO Publishing Company, 4940 Viking Drive, Suite 622, Edina, Minnesota 55435. Copyright ©2003 by Abdo Consulting Group, Inc. International copyrights reserved in all countries. No part of this book may be reproduced in any form without written permission from the publisher.

Printed in the United States.

Edited by Paul Joseph
Graphic Design: John Hamilton
Cover Design: Mighty Media
Photos and illustrations:
    John Hamilton, p. 4, 5, 7, 9, 10, 13, 14, 15, 17, 20, 22, 23, 24, 25, 26, 27, 30
    American Philosophical Society, p. 16
    Beinecke Museum, p. 8
    Buffalo Bill Historical Society, William Jacob Hays, p. 1
    George Catlin, p. 18, 21, 29
    Library of Congress, W. Clark, E.S. Curtis, p. 3, 19, 20, 28, 30-31
    Missouri Bankers Association, L. Edward Fisher, p. 12
    Charles Willson Peale, p. 6, 7
    St. Charles County Historical Society, Morganthaler, p. 11

Library of Congress Cataloging-in-Publication Data

Hamilton, John, 1959-
    The Missouri River / John Hamilton.
    p. cm.—(Lewis & Clark)
    Includes bibliographical references and index.
    Summary: Joins the Lewis and Clark Expedition from the time it leaves camp near St. Louis in the spring of 1804 to travel up the Missouri River until its members settle for the winter near present-day Bismarck, North Dakota. Includes highlights and directions to historical points of interest.
    ISBN 1-57765-762-4
    1. Lewis and Clark Expedition (1804-1806)—Juvenile literature. 2. West (U.S.)—Discovery and exploration—Juvenile literature. 3. West (U.S.)—Description and travel—Juvenile literature. 4. Missouri River—Description and travel—Juvenile literature. [1. Lewis and Clark Expedition (1804-1806) 2. West (U.S.)—Discovery and exploration. 3. Missouri River—Description and travel.] I. Title.

F592.7.H27 2002
917.804'2—dc21

2001053401

Table of Contents

"*Dear Captain Lewis,*
"*The acquisition of the country through which you are to pass has inspired the public generally with a great deal of interest in your enterprize... Present my salutations to Mr. Clarke, assure all your party that we have our eyes turned on them with anxiety for their safety.*"
THOMAS JEFFERSON

MAKE READY

*I*n December of 1803, Meriwether Lewis and William Clark set up camp on the Illinois side of the Mississippi River, just upstream from St. Louis. On the opposite shore, the Missouri River emptied into the Mississippi. The explorers constructed several huts, which they called Camp Dubois (also called Camp Wood). When the camp was finished, they settled in for the winter to collect supplies and train their men for the journey to come.

The Lewis and Clark expedition would be the first official exploration of unknown lands to the northwest, in a huge territory known as Louisiana. (Today's state of Louisiana is just a small part of the former territory.) Maps of North America pictured Louisiana as a huge blank area. Nobody knew for sure what was out there.

Several countries wanted to control Louisiana. France, England, and Spain had already attempted to explore its vast reaches. Besides rich potential in fur trapping and minerals, they were also looking for an easy trade route to the Pacific Ocean, the fabled Northwest Passage.

Although claimed by Spain, and then France, the territory was still in dispute. Whoever explored Louisiana controlled it. And whoever controlled Louisiana controlled the destiny of the North American continent. The United States was a young country in 1803, having declared independence less than three decades earlier. There were only 17 states. The country's mastery of the continent was far from certain.

Meriwether Lewis was 28 years old when President Thomas Jefferson picked him to lead the Corps of Discovery. The Corps (pronounced *core*) would be a military mission to explore Louisiana for the United States. Jefferson also wanted Lewis to cross the Rocky Mountains and find an easy trade route to the Pacific Ocean via the Columbia River system.

Lewis, a fellow Virginia plantation owner, had been Jefferson's personal secretary in Washington, D.C., for two years. He was an army captain, a superb woodsman, intelligent, and a fast learner. He could fall into dark moods, but always managed to set his problems aside in order to get the job done. President Jefferson had every confidence in his young protégé.

Lewis picked his good friend William Clark to help lead the Corps of Discovery. Clark, a former army captain, had once been Lewis's commander. He was a sturdy man with flaming red hair. Like Lewis, he was a seasoned woodsman. He spent time on the wild frontiers of Kentucky and Ohio, learning to fight and negotiate with Native Americans. Four years older than Lewis, Clark was steadier and more outgoing. Although less educated, Clark had more practical experience and was more even-tempered. He was a perfect complement to Lewis.

Technically, Clark was a lieutenant on the expedition. Lewis kept this fact a secret from the other men, and always referred to his friend as Captain Clark. They were co-commanders throughout the journey.

Meriwether Lewis, in a painting by Charles Willson Peale.

Lewis & Clark

On July 4, 1803, President Jefferson announced the Louisiana Purchase. He had bought 820,000 square miles (2,123,798 sq km) from France for $15 million, only three cents an acre. The sale nearly doubled the size of the United States. As the Corps of Discovery traveled up the Missouri River, it would now be exploring American territory.

On July 5, Meriwether Lewis started down the Ohio River. Near Pittsburgh he had a large keelboat built to carry men and cargo. When it was finished, Lewis sailed downstream, picking up Clark and eager recruits along the way to St. Louis.

In the winter, the Corps could not travel. The snow was too deep, it was too cold, and there wasn't enough game to hunt. After settling in at Camp Dubois to wait out the winter of 1803-1804, Clark began training the men. Most were soldiers, since this was to be a military expedition. Finding volunteers was no problem. With the added promise of money and land, the expedition would be the trip of a lifetime.

William Clark, painted by Charles Willson Peale.

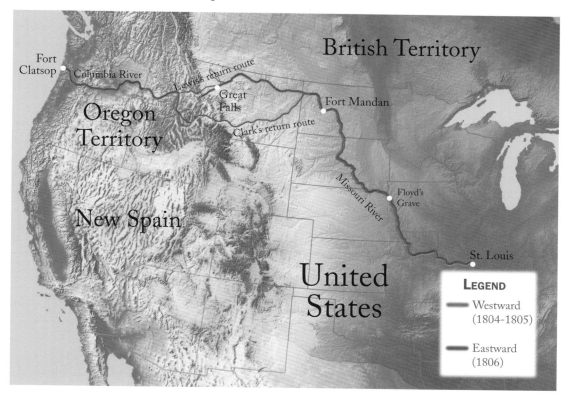

THE KEELBOAT

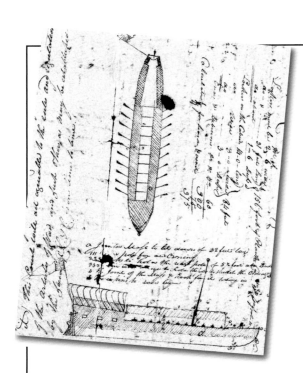

Keelboats are large, flat-bottomed freight boats once common on the Mississippi and Missouri Rivers. Clark's journal (left) shows the expedition's keelboat. It was 55 feet (16.8 m) long, and 8 feet (2.4 m) wide. The stern (back) held a small cabin with windows, with a deck on top. The bow (front) had a small cannon, or swivel gun, which could quickly be turned in any direction.

The center of the keelboat was the cargo area, which held 10 tons (9 metric tons) of supplies. More cargo was held in lockers along the sides of the boat. These had wooden lids that could be raised to protect the men if they were attacked.

Twenty oars powered the keelboat. It also had a mast, on which two sails could be raised if the wind was at the explorers' backs. The Missouri River was sometimes too shallow to row such a big boat. On such occasions, men with long poles pushed against the river bottom and walked toward the back of the boat, inching the vessel forward. Sometimes even this didn't work, and the men had to resort to *cordelling* or trudging on shore and pulling the boat with heavy ropes.

The men came from all corners of the United States, and from all walks of life. Lewis wrote that they were looking for "Stout, healthy, unmarried men, accustomed to the woods, and capable of bearing bodily fatigue."

Charles Floyd was a 22-year-old soldier from Kentucky. "A young man of much merit," Lewis wrote. Charles Floyd and Nathaniel Pryor were cousins. Reubin and Joseph Field were brothers. John Ordway was a young man from Hebron, New Hampshire. John Shields, at 35, the oldest enlisted man, was an expert blacksmith. Joseph Whitehouse was a tailor from Virginia, Patrick Gass a carpenter from Pennsylvania. The youngest man was George Shannon, who turned 19 in 1804.

Clark brought along a man named York. He was an African-American slave who had been with Clark since childhood. During the journey, the big man would prove his worth many times, becoming an important part of the Corps.

Lewis also brought a Newfoundland dog, called Seaman. The dog, which weighed nearly 150 pounds (68 kg), helped hunt and guard the camp. Seaman was quick to fetch squirrels, geese, and beaver for his master. He even once ran down a deer that had been wounded by a hunter.

The Corps also employed several civilians. George Drouillard (pronounced *Drew-yer*) was the son of a French-Canadian father and Shawnee Indian mother. He was a skilled hunter, knew the lower Missouri River, and could speak the sign language of the Plains Indians.

Clark drilled the volunteers during their five-month stay at Camp Dubois. He prepared them to work as a team. He carefully noted who best followed orders, who was the strongest, who was the quickest, and who had the most endurance. He looked for men with good carpentry and metalworking skills, and noted the best hunters.

Lewis, meanwhile, spent time across the river in St. Louis gathering last-minute supplies. In 1803, St. Louis was a frontier town with less than 1,500 people. Lewis questioned trappers and explorers who had ventured partway up the Missouri. He learned enough to have a rough idea of what they would find, at least until they reached the Mandan Indian villages in present-day North Dakota. No American citizen had ever ventured beyond that point.

Camp Dubois, on the Illinois side of the Mississippi River. Because the river channel has shifted over the years, it is only an approximate location of the Corps's winter quarters of 1803-04.

"Monday 14th May 1804 hard Showers of rain. This being the day appointed by Capt. Clark to Set out... we fired our Swivel on the bow hoisted Sail and Set out in high Spirits for the western Expedition."

JOSEPH WHITEHOUSE

UNDERWAY

O n May 14, 1804, the Corps of Discovery—nearly four-dozen strong—set off from Camp Dubois. The keelboat and two canoe-like pirogues, one red, one white, crossed the Mississippi—"Under a jentle brease," wrote William Clark—and entered the mouth of the Missouri River. With Clark on deck, they finally left their dreary winter quarters behind and started the expedition for which they had waited so long.

Clark was in a cheerful mood that day. Below him on the main deck, 20 men strained in unison at their oars, rowing against the muddy current of the Missouri. They traveled four and a half miles (seven km) that first day, stopping at the small French town of St. Charles. Meriwether Lewis, who had been in St. Louis picking up last-minute supplies, hurried his horse through a fierce thunderstorm to meet the expedition. The citizens of St. Charles threw a festive party in honor of the Corps. After being cooped up in winter camp for so long, the men were happy to relax and have some fun.

On May 25, the Corps passed by the settlement of La Charette, an outpost of seven small huts. Sergeant Charles Floyd wrote in his journal that it was "the last settlement of whites on this river." They were now beyond the reaches of Western civilization.

This early painting by Charles A. Morganthaler shows the Corps as it departs from St. Charles. The keelboat is incorrectly shown with a front cabin.

This painting by L. Edward Fisher shows the keelboat and the two pirogues as they pass the forested bluffs of the lower Missouri River in May, 1804.

The landscape of the lower Missouri River was beautiful to behold, with wildflowers and fruit trees dotting the shoreline. Forested limestone bluffs rose up on either side, covered with hardwood trees in full spring bloom. Ducks, wild birds, and frogs added a chorus of song to the humid air.

Travel up the river was slow. Today, dams tame the Missouri. In 1804, however, the river was still wild. Currents were unpredictable. Churning, muddy water hid rocks and sandbars. Fallen trees, called snags, were swept downriver, sometimes lurking just under the brown water. Maneuvering the huge keelboat was always a challenge. Once it got hung up on a snag and nearly overturned.

The Missouri River was very swift. The men had to row five miles per hour (eight km/h) just to stay even with the current. They avoided the main channel, shifting from eddy to eddy, looking for relatively still water. Sometimes overhanging trees along shore snagged the keelboat's mast, snapping it in two.

On a good day, the expedition could travel 14 miles (23 km). When the wind was at their backs, they could hoist sails and get a boost. More often, though, they had to use poles to push against the river bottom, or pull the boats by rope, either in the shallows or along the banks. It was backbreaking work. Thunderstorms often forced them to stop. After two months, they were still in what is now the state of Missouri.

An actor portraying George Drouillard, hired by Lewis and Clark as a hunter and Native American interpreter.

"May 29th. Rained last night... The Musquetors are verry bad. Made 4 miles."

WILLIAM CLARK

WE PROCEEDED ON

As the Corps of Discovery made its way up the Missouri River, some men rowed or pulled the boats. Others hunted for game along the shore. The men used so much energy rowing and pulling that they ate seven to nine pounds (3 to 4 kg) of meat each day just to keep up their strength. The expedition's best hunter was George Drouillard, who was an expert marksman. Lewis wrote in his journals, "I scarcely know how we should subsist were it not for the exertions of this excellent hunter."

William Clark spent most of his time on the keelboat, taking compass readings and measuring distances for a map he would later draw for Thomas Jefferson.

Lewis often walked or rode his horse on shore, helping hunt game or making notes about the plants and animals they saw. Soon after leaving St. Charles, Lewis climbed a limestone cliff. He slipped and almost fell 300 feet (91 m) to his death. Clark wrote that Lewis "Saved himself by the assistance of his Knife... he caught at 20 foot."

An actor pilots a replica of the Corps of Discovery's keelboat. Two blunderbusses are mounted on each side of the deck.

The Journals

One of the reasons we know so much about the Corps of Discovery is that Lewis and Clark kept daily journals. The captains recorded each day's events in their elkskin-covered notebooks, noting the plants and animals they came across, the weather, American Indians they encountered, and anything else worthy of notice. Lewis and Clark insisted that other men of the Corps keep journals also, in case the captains' journals were lost or damaged. Patrick Gass, Charles Floyd, John Ordway, and Joseph Whitehouse were among those who kept their own journals. Their notes help fill in the gaps of captains' journals, giving us a more complete picture of the expedition.

Something you might notice when reading the journals is the misspelled words. Back in those days, there was no standardized spelling—it would be another 24 years before Noah Webster published his first dictionary. Journal writers simply wrote phonetically, spelling words as they thought they sounded. For example, the word *mosquito* appears in the journals in many different ways, including musquetor, musqutor, musquitoe, misqueter, musquetoe, and musketoe.

Insects were a constant misery. Armies of ticks dug into the men's flesh, and mosquitoes swarmed around their faces. Lewis wrote that mosquitoes were "so numerous that we frequently get them in our throats as we breathe." The men smeared bear grease on their bodies to keep the pests at bay. At night they used mosquito netting that Lewis had brought.

In the evening, the Corps broke up into three squads, each led by its own sergeant. Each squad did its own cooking, cleaning, and repairing of equipment. Evening also gave them a chance to rest their weary bodies. Many of the men got sick, or had bad shoulders and joints. Some suffered from snakebites. Their drinking water came from the muddy Missouri, which gave them diarrhea. Lewis tended to the men with his knowledge of medicine and herbal healing.

The journey was difficult, but the men were young and tough, and their spirits remained high. They marked the first Fourth of July ever celebrated west of the Mississippi River by firing the keelboat's cannon.

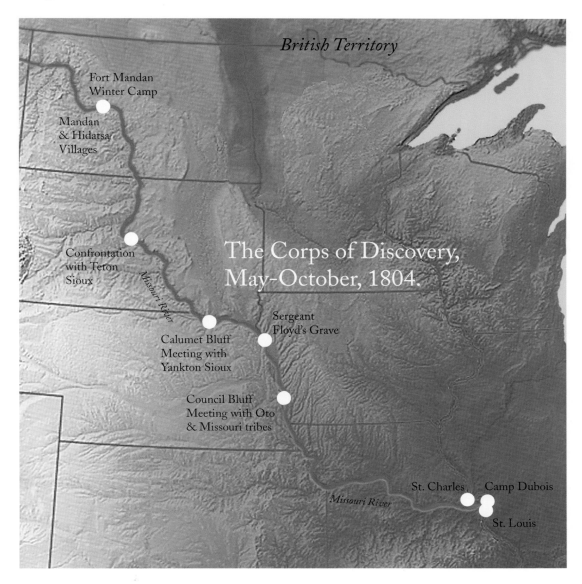

British Territory

Fort Mandan
Winter Camp

Mandan
& Hidatsa
Villages

Confrontation
with Teton
Sioux

Missouri River

The Corps of Discovery,
May–October, 1804.

Calumet Bluff
Meeting with
Yankton Sioux

Sergeant
Floyd's Grave

Council Bluff
Meeting with Oto
& Missouri tribes

St. Charles   Camp Dubois

Missouri River

St. Louis

"The best authenticated accounts informed us, that we were to pass through a country possessed by numerous, powerful and warlike nations of savages, of gigantic stature, fierce, treacherous and cruel; and particularly hostile to white men."
PATRICK GASS

"My heart is gladder than it ever was before to see [a white man]. If you want to open the road, no one can prevent it. It will always be open to you."
KAKAWISSASSA, LIGHTNING CROW

THE PRAIRIE TRIBES

Lewis and Clark were under orders by Thomas Jefferson to contact as many Native American tribes as possible. Jefferson was especially interested in setting up fur-trading partnerships. He knew that trade and commerce would encourage people to settle into the new territories, expanding the reach of the United States.

Jefferson also had a scientific curiosity about Native Americans. He ordered Lewis and Clark to study their languages, cultures, and customs.

During the first part of their journey, there were few Indian encounters. The tribes were out on the Great Plains, hunting buffalo. Finally, on August 3, 1804, the Corps had its first meeting with western Indians near present-day Omaha, Nebraska. They met for a day with members of the Oto and Missouri Indian tribes at a place Clark called "Council Bluff."

Painted lodges of the Plains Indians, photographed by Edward S. Curtis.

Lewis and Clark had a routine for meeting with the Native Americans. Dressed in their finest uniforms and three-cornered hats, they first told the Indians that they had a new "White Father" (Thomas Jefferson). Then they displayed modern technology, such as rifles, magnets, and spyglasses. The men paraded and marched in military formation, firing volleys from their rifles. Lewis demonstrated his specially built air rifle, which greatly impressed the Indians.

They handed out presents, representing the wealth of the United States. The gifts included beads, flags, vermilion, knives, tobacco, and special peace medals for the Indian chiefs. The medals had a portrait of Thomas Jefferson engraved on one side, and two hands clasped in friendship on the other.

Lastly, Lewis and Clark urged the Indians to stop making war against their neighbors, and to make the United States their trade partner. They promised peace and prosperity if they did as they were told.

White people had been trading on the lower Missouri for nearly a century before Lewis and Clark passed through. The Native Americans had heard this kind of arrogant talk before. It was very insulting to be told that the land they had occupied for generations was suddenly "owned" by an unseen "White Father" in the East.

Still, most of the Indians who encountered Lewis and Clark on the Missouri were eager to start a trade partnership. They wanted metal tools to make their lives easier, and they wanted weapons to give them an advantage over their neighbors.

The front and back of the peace medals Lewis and Clark gave to Native American chiefs.

Plains Indians photographed by Edward S. Curtis 100 years after the Lewis and Clark expedition.

A George Catlin painting of a Plains Indian hunting buffalo.

"August 20ᵗʰ. Sergeant Floyd much weaker and no better... No pulse & nothing will stay a moment on his Stomach... Passed two Islands, and at the first Bluff on the starboard side, Sgt. Floyd Died with a great deal of composure; before his death he Said to me, "I am going away. I want you to write me a letter."

WILLIAM CLARK

On August 20, 1804, near present-day Sioux City, Iowa, Sergeant Charles Floyd died. Lewis wrote that he passed away from "bilious cholic." Historians think Floyd probably suffered a burst appendix. Even if he had been safely back home, nothing could have saved him—doctors didn't yet know how to perform appendectomies.

Floyd was buried on a bluff overlooking the Missouri River. His grave is marked today by a giant stone monument. Floyd was the first U.S. soldier to die west of the Mississippi River, and was the only fatality of the Corps of Discovery.

On August 30, the Corps met with a group of friendly Yankton Sioux Indians at a place called Calumet Bluff. Clark, who was always more at ease among the Native Americans than Lewis, called the Yanktons a "stout, bold looking people."

The meeting was a success. The Yankton chiefs agreed to more trade with the Americans. One chief even agreed to travel east to meet with President Jefferson.

But the chiefs had a warning for Lewis and Clark. Chief Half Man told them that the next tribe upriver would not be so friendly. These, the chief said, were the powerful and feared Teton Sioux, the Lakotas, and they "will not open their ears, and you cannot, I fear, open them."

"*There is no timber in this part of the country; but continued prairie on both sides of the river. A person by going on one of the hills may have a view as far as the eye can reach without any obstruction; and enjoy the most delightful prospects.*"

PATRICK GASS

THE GREAT PLAINS

By September of 1804, the Corps had moved onto the Great Plains, the largest grassland of the world. The only trees hugged the river bottom; beyond that, there was nothing but grassland, rolling hills that stretched to the horizon.

The men could see vast herds of wildlife—elk, deer, and buffalo by the thousands. There were wolves and owls, ducks and frogs, hawks and grouse. The immense open plains stunned the explorers. It was like a vast Garden of Eden. It was especially surprising because they had lived their whole lives in wooded areas. A common saying at the time was that a squirrel could jump from tree to tree all the way to the Mississippi River. But at the Great Plains, the squirrel stopped.

Lewis and Clark began cataloguing plants and animals that were unknown back home, and new to science: coyotes, mules, deer, jackrabbits. They were the first to describe pronghorn, the fastest animal in North America, clocked at over 70 miles per hour (113 km/h). Native Americans knew these animals, of course, and fur trappers had seen them before. But the journals of Lewis and Clark were the first detailed descriptions of these "curiousities," as the captains called them.

Pronghorn grazing on the plains of South Dakota.

Prairie dogs on the plains of North Dakota.

"I have called [it] the barking squirrel... It's form is that of the squirrel... [but] they bark at you as you approach them, their note being much that of little toy dogs... It is much more quick active and fleet than it's form would indicate."

MERIWETHER LEWIS

On September 7, the Corps discovered "barking squirrels," or as John Ordway called them, prairie dogs. The entire expedition struggled for hours to capture one. They finally succeeded by pouring water down its hole and flushing it out. The prairie dog was caged and eventually sent back live to a delighted President Jefferson, along with several boxes of skins and plant specimens.

In late August, Private George Shannon, the youngest member of the Corps, got lost while hunting on the Plains. He eventually made it back to the river, but found nobody there. He thought the expedition had left without him, so he hurried upstream, trying to catch up. Actually, the rest of the men were behind Shannon!

After two weeks on his own, the lost teenager finally sat down on the riverbank, hoping that a fur-trading boat might someday pick him up. The Corps eventually caught up to Shannon and found him there, starving and weak. He had run out of bullets, living on nothing but a rabbit and some wild grapes.

Clark later wrote in his journal, "Thus a man had like to have Starved to death in a land of Plenty for the want of Bullitts or Something to kill his meat."

A snake hunts for food on the bluffs overlooking the Missouri River in North Dakota.

"You will probably meet with parties of [the Teton Sioux]. On that nation we wish most particularly to make a friendly impression, because of their immense power."

THOMAS JEFFERSON

CLOSE CALL

On September 25, 1804, the Corps of Discovery finally encountered a band of Teton Sioux—the Lakotas—at the mouth of the Bad River, near today's Pierre, South Dakota. The Lakotas were a powerful group, and hostile to their neighbors and the few whites who traveled through their territory. Fur trappers called them the bullies of the Missouri River.

Lewis and Clark gave their usual Indian speech and demonstration, but their audience was unimpressed. The Lakotas controlled river traffic and the trade of their neighbors. The Corps of Discovery's mission threatened to distrupt their monopoly on trade. It threatened their way of life.

The Lakotas demanded more gifts. They also told the Corps that they would not be allowed to travel any farther upriver. Lewis and Clark arranged for three of the Teton Sioux chiefs to tour the expedition's keelboat. After the tour, the chiefs were still hostile. Clark took them back to shore in one of the pirogues. Then the situation worsened.

Warriors grabbed the pirogue's tow rope. One of the chiefs got into a heated argument with Clark. The captain drew his sword. Warriors along the riverbank nocked their arrows, ready to fire.

The site where Lewis and Clark first met the Teton Sioux, at the intersection of the Missouri and Bad Rivers, near present-day Pierre, South Dakota.

"Capt Clark Spoke to all the party to Stand to their arms. Capt Lewis who was on board [the keelboat] ordered every man to his arms. The large Swivel [gun was] loaded immediately with 16 Musquet balls in it, the 2 other Swivels loaded well with Buck Shot [and] each of them manned. Capt Clark... told them that we must and would go on; that we were not Squaws, but warriers.

"The chief sayed he had warriers too and if we were to go on they would follow us and kill and take the whole of us by degrees."

JOHN ORDWAY

It was a tense moment, one that could easily have ended in disaster, with many killed on each side. Instead, a Lakota chief, Black Buffalo, wisely defused the crisis. He changed the subject and requested only that the women and children of his village be allowed to visit the keelboat before the Corps moved on.

After three tense days among the Lakotas, the Corps departed, happy to put some distance between themselves and the "bullies of the Missouri."

In early October, the men encountered members of the Arikara tribe. They had once numbered almost 30,000, but 20 years earlier a smallpox epidemic killed nine of ten Arikara. On October 8, the Corps met the survivors, who were much friendlier than the Teton Sioux.

Hollow Horn Bear, from the Brulé band of the Teton Sioux, photographed by Edward S. Curtis.

*"October 21ˢᵗ. We had a disagreeable night of sleet and hail.
It snowed during the forenoon, but we proceeded early on our voyage."*
PATRICK GASS

A Sioux council, painted by George Catlin.

The days of October shortened and grew cold. Huge flocks of birds flew overhead on their migration south. In what is now North Dakota, Clark estimated they had traveled 1,600 miles (2,575 km) up the Missouri River.

They had hoped to make it to the river's headwaters by now, but they weren't even close. With winter fast approaching, the captains knew they had to stop soon to build a fort and prepare for cold weather. They decided to stop at the Mandan Indian villages, the last known point on their maps. That spring they would venture into unknown lands. But first, they had to survive a harsh, bone-chilling winter on the Great Plains.

IF YOU GO TODAY

ST. LOUIS, MISSOURI

The city of St. Louis hosts a number of sites relating to Lewis and Clark. Under the Gateway Arch (left) is the Museum of Westward Expansion, which has large collections of exhibits and photographs related to the Corps of Discovery. The

Missouri Historical Society has four floors of exhibits on Lewis and Clark, Indian culture, and the westward migration of early pioneers. Bellefontaine Cemetery (right) is the final resting place of William Clark, and other historical figures.

LEWIS AND CLARK STATE PARK

On a small oxbow lake about five miles (8 km) west of the town of Onawa, Iowa, is a full-scale copy of the expedition's keelboat. There are also reproductions of the two pirogues that traveled along up the Missouri River.

SERGEANT FLOYD MONUMENT

Sergeant Floyd, the only fatality of the Corps of Discovery, is buried on a bluff overlooking the Missouri River near Sioux City, Iowa. The grave is marked with a tall obelisk. Informative plaques tell the story of the expedition.

Also in Sioux City, at the Sergeant Floyd Riverboat Museum, are 19th century photographs of Floyd's grave, copies of Clark's maps, and other items from the expedition.

GLOSSARY

CORPS

A branch of the military that has a specialized function.

GREAT PLAINS

A huge, sloping region of valleys and plains in west-central North America. The Great Plains extend from Texas to southern Canada, and from the Rocky Mountains nearly 400 miles (644 km) to the east.

KEELBOAT

A large, shallow-hulled freight boat used extensively in the 18th and 19th centuries on the Mississippi and Missouri Rivers.

NORTHWEST PASSAGE

The fabled easy water route across North America from the Atlantic to the Pacific Ocean.

PIROGUE

A large, canoe-shaped boat, used to carry cargo, that is powered by oars, or sometimes a sail. The Corps of Discovery used two pirogues.

PLAINS INDIANS

Native Americans who lived on the Great Plains of North America. They spoke different languages, but shared many cultural traits, such as a nomadic following of bison herds.

WEB SITES

Would you like to learn more about Lewis & Clark? Please visit **www.abdopub.com** to find up-to-date Web site links about Lewis & Clark and the Corps of Discovery. These links are routinely monitored and updated to provide the most current information available.

INDEX